9/96

J A/994

Garrett, Dan
(9/96

Garrett, Dan J/994
Australia

2314

OCT 14 2008

Y0-EKA-190

VAN BUREN PUBLIC LIBRARY
VAN BUREN, IND.
RULES

1. Books may be kept for two weeks and may be renewed once for the same period, except 7 day books and magazines.

117329 Australia

VAN BUREN PUBLIC LIBRARY

World in view
Australia

Dan Garrett & Warrill Grindrod

STECK-VAUGHN
LIBRARY
Austin, Texas

Published in the United States in 1990 by Steck-Vaughn Co., Austin, Texas, a subsidiary of National Education Corporation.

© Macmillan Publishers Limited 1989

All rights reserved. No reproduction, copy or transmission of this publication may be made without written permission.

First published 1989

Published by Macmillan Children's Books
A division of MACMILLAN PUBLISHERS LTD

Designed by Julian Holland Publishing Ltd.
Picture research by Jennifer Johnson

Library of Congress Cataloging-in-Publication Data

Garrett, Dan, 1941–
  Australia.

  (World in view)
  "First published 1989. Published by Macmillan Children's Books"—T.p. verso.
  Includes index.
  Summary: Surveys the geography, history, agriculture, city life, leisure activities, education and health programs, and outdoor lifestyle of Australia.
  I. Grindrod, Warrill, 1953–   .II. Title.
  III. Series.
  DU96.G37   1989   944   89-21726
  ISBN 0-8114-2429-4

Printed and bound in the United States.
   2 3 4 5 6 7 8 9 0 LB 94 93 92 91

Acknowledgments
Thanks to the many people and organizations who helped us in Australia, including many friends and colleagues in the different offices of the ABC, the Anglican Church in Australia, as well as Julie Foster, Sally Greaves, Chris Weston, and many other friends and relatives.

Photographic credits
Cover: A. Caulfield/The Image Bank (Dallas), title page: Warrill Grindrod, 8 Australian Overseas Information Service, London (AOIS), 11 Barry Le Lievre/AOIS, 15, 16, 17 Bruce Coleman Ltd, 20 Northern Territory Tourist Commission, 26 National Library of Australia, 28 AOIS, 29 e.t. archives, 30 Mary Evans Picture Library, 33, 34 Topham, 36 AOIS, 38 Axel Poignant Archive, 40 AOIS, 43 SYDAIP, 45 Compix, 46, G. Sherlock, 47 Axel Poignant Archive, 48 AOIS, 49 Picturepoint, 51/50 J. Allan Cash, 53 South Australia State Promotion Unit, 54 AOIS, 56 G. Sherlock, 60, 67 Warrill Grindrod, 68, 72 AOIS, 76 Northern Territory Tourist Commission, 77 Keith Job/Hutchinson Library, 79 Dan Garrett, 81 AOIS, 82 Picturepoint, 85 Australian Tourist Commission, 87 South Australia Government Tourist Bureau, 88 Warrill Grindrod, 89 Dave Saunders, 92 Allsport/Ozsport.

Contents

1. A Country With a Continent to Itself 5
2. Before the Europeans 13
3. Explorers, Convicts, and Settlers 21
4. Independent Australia 31
5. Bullocks, Camels, and Qantas 37
6. A Living From the Land 44
7. Opals, Gold, and Iron Mountains 52
8. Cities 59
9. Australians 66
10. The Sky Is Our Church 74
11. Learning and Caring 79
12. Outdoor Lifestyle 85
    Index 94

AUSTRALIA

1 A Country With a Continent to Itself

It takes a long time to fly to Australia. From New York's Kennedy Airport to Sydney, Australia, the journey lasts more than 24 hours. Even from California it's a long way, more than 13 hours right across the Pacific. By modern standards the journey can be very tiring, but in the days of sailing boats, ships' captains thought they were doing well if they managed to sail the 12,000 miles from London to Sydney in less than three months.

The distance to Australia means that travelers go through many time zones. When it's Monday noon in Sydney, it is nine o'clock on Sunday evening in New York. The times change depending on when Australian and American daylight saving start each year.

Such time distances have strange effects. A young person in Chicago can cheerfully decide at noon to phone cousins in Australia, only to find that they're in bed. A business executive in Sydney can send a fax message late on Monday afternoon explaining what has been done during the day. In New York a colleague gets the printout first thing on the same Monday morning when he comes in to work. People can feel as if they are in a time machine.

Most countries share a continent with other countries. Australia is unique because it has a continent to itself: it's like an immense island on the southwestern edge of the Pacific Ocean. Its

AUSTRALIA

Australia is divided into six self-governing states and two territories. The capital of Australia is Canberra in the Australian Capital Territory. There are also extended territories such as Australian Antarctic Territory.

near neighbors are New Zealand to the southeast and New Guinea to the north. Further northward are Southeast Asia, China, and Japan.

Our picture of Australia as a land of endless sunshine is very nearly true, and one of the reasons is its nearness to the equator. Even Hobart in the extreme south of Australia, is only as far from the equator as northern Spain. The result is that Australia has a range of climates from tropical in northern Queensland to temperate in the southern island of Tasmania.

A COUNTRY WITH A CONTINENT TO ITSELF

The land
Australia is one of the oldest and certainly the flattest of continents. Its average height above sea level is less than 1,000 feet. It has one major mountain range, the Great Dividing Range, stretching down the eastern side, 30 to 200 miles inland. With heights up to 7,000 feet it is not a high range in comparison with the U.S.'s Rocky Mountains, the European Alps, or the Himalayas. The highest peaks are only about a quarter the height of Mount Everest.

Australia's highest point: Mount Kosciusko, 7,316 feet
Australia's lowest point: Lake Eyre, 39 feet below sea level
Longest river: The Darling 1,700 miles
Australia is as big as Europe, or the United States without Alaska.

Australia's flag has a dark blue background and shows the stars of the Southern Cross and the southern pole stars. These stars are only visible in the southern hemisphere. In the top left-hand corner is the Union flag to show Australia's early links with Great Britain.

The currency is the Australian dollar shown by A$. It is a decimal system, so the dollar is divided into 100 cents. This system was introduced in 1966. Coins are issued in 1, 2, 5, 10, 20, and 50 cents and $1. Paper money is also used, of which the highest is $100.

AUSTRALIA

Until it was returned to the Aboriginal people, Uluru was named Ayers Rock. It rises out of a flat plain, and the red-brown rock, which changes color as the day passes, can be seen from many miles away.

Apart from the Great Dividing Range, there are only a few small mountain ranges around 3,300 feet high. Very noticeable, particularly from the air, are strange mountainous rock formations like the Olgas in the Northern Territory. Near the Olgas is Australia's most famous landmark. Uluru, or Ayers Rock as it used to be known, is a great red rock rising spectacularly 1,100 feet out of flat semidesert.

Many of these strange rock formations are related to mineral deposits. Australia has many rare minerals such as gold, diamonds, opals, and uranium. It also has huge reserves of iron and aluminum ore and coal. (See Chapter 7.)

A COUNTRY WITH A CONTINENT TO ITSELF

The bush and the outback
These two words are often heard in Australia. The bush is the name for countryside that is either thickly or thinly wooded. The thickly wooded areas of the Blue Mountains are called the bush and so are the areas farther inland where trees are thinly spread across grassland. Geographers call this landscape savannah. For Australians it's still the bush.

Most of the center of Australia is desert, or semidesert. It is these thinly populated areas that Australians call the outback.

It's very easy to fall into the trap of believing that all Australians live an outback life. In fact, 14 million out of Australia's total population of 16 million live in towns and cities. This makes it one of the most urbanized of modern societies. Relatively few Australians fit the outback image of living miles away from their nearest neighbor on isolated ranches.

The weather
Australia's closeness to the equator is the reason for its high temperatures. Most rain falls around the coast where winds pick up moisture from the sea. The tropical northern and northeast coasts have the highest rainfall, 40 - 80 inches per year, and surprisingly these figures are also reached on the storm-swept western ranges of Tasmania. Even Sydney's rainfall is 40 inches which is as high as the average rainfall along the east coast of the United States.

Inland, however, Australia is very dry, one of the driest places in the world. Averages of less than six inches per year mask extremely irregular

AUSTRALIA

Average temperatures	summer	winter
Cape York (northern Queensland)	84°F	77°F
Tasmania (southeastern Australia)	63°F	46°F

Highest Sydney temperature ever: 114°F
Highest shade temperature: 128°F (Cloncurry, Queensland 1889)
Hottest climate: Marble Bar, in the northwest of Western Australia — temperatures over 120°F are common

rainfall. People may go seven years without seeing rain, and then experience a deluge in which 12 inches may fall in 12 hours. Rainfall like this can act as a trigger and suddenly, spectacularly and wonderfully, the desert blooms. Small animals hidden during the drought seem to come to life from nowhere. Such a climate makes farming very difficult and risky. Drought destroys crops and often puts farmers out of business.

The rainfall patterns and the flatness of the country mean that Australia has, for its size, very few rivers. Most of these are short in comparison with great river systems elsewhere, like the Mississippi River or the Amazon in Brazil. There is actually only one large river system, the Murray-Darling. With the Murrumbidgee and other tributaries, the combined rivers drain most of southeastern Australia, about one-eighth of the continent.

Australia's climate makes it rivers unreliable, and they often dry up. Some rivers such as the

A COUNTRY WITH A CONTINENT TO ITSELF

Diamantina in Queensland flow inland, and for a long time early explorers expected to find an inland sea. The climate is so hot that there are only salt lakes like Lake Eyre in South Australia, dry most of the time because evaporation is greater than the river flow.

Natural hazards
As well as irregular rainfall, Australians have to cope with other fearsome natural hazards. The tropical north coast is often swept by cyclones,

More than half of Darwin's 12,000 houses and apartments were destroyed when Cyclone Tracy flattened the city. Winds gusted to 175 miles per hour.

AUSTRALIA

which are tropical storms with heavy rain and strong whirling winds. They can cause immense damage and one especially, Cyclone Tracy, flattened the city of Darwin in 1974.

Particularly on the north and east coasts, Australians also learn to expect flash floods. Even a city is not safe, and in 1974 Brisbane was flooded after five days of rain.

Elsewhere, the dry climate and the oily leaves of the gum trees make bush fires a common hazard. One of the worst recent fires was in Victoria and South Australia on Ash Wednesday 1983. A wall of flames spread 750 miles across the two states, leaping roads, and threatening cities. A fire on that scale in the United States would spread from Detroit to Atlanta.

Dust storms are another hazard. Modern intensive farming methods have removed many of the trees and shrubs that bind the thin soil. When there is drought, winds whip up the soil into a choking dust-cloud that can travel long distances. In 1983, one huge dust storm covered most of Melbourne with thick red dust.

Despite these sudden catastrophes, the weather is usually pleasant and Australians enjoy an outdoor lifestyle.

2 Before the Europeans

Many millions of years before there were human beings in Australia, it was much farther south than it is today. Australia was joined to Antarctica, as were Africa and South America. Then, amazingly, this whole land mass began to split up. It is like the skin on top of warm custard being pushed around into different places. Something similar happened to Australia. It split away from Antarctica, and over millions of years moved north to its present position. As it split away, it took its own evolving wildlife with it. This is why Australian plants and animals are very special, and in many ways quite different from plants and animals on other continents.

Trees...
Over millions of years, Australia's climate changed and became drier. The forest of trees, which originally covered the whole land, found it harder to survive. In many places the tree cover died out altogether to leave large deserts like Sturts Desert or the Great Victoria Desert. In other parts, forests were replaced with open scrub, or grassland with scattered trees, a savannah type of landscape. In Queensland, some of the original rain forests still survive.

The unpredictability of the rainfall meant that plants had to evolve to cope with long periods of drought. Some did it by creating massive root systems which survived even when the leaves and branches had withered. Mallee scrub is one of this type. Other plants evolved their own private water tanks. Bottle trees have massively thick stems that fill with water when it rains. Some plants developed underground tubers from which new growth could spring up after rainfall. Others evolved very hard seeds that could survive years of drought without rotting.

The gum tree, or eucalyptus is special to Australia. It is very recognizable by its peeling bark and blue-green leaves. These are long and hard and droop vertically away from the sun in order to conserve water. There are over 500 varieties of gum tree, all with the dry pungent smell of eucalyptus oil.

. . . and the animals in them
Gum leaves are poisonous to many species of animals, but koalas have found a way of digesting them. Their stomaches contain a special bacteria which has to be passed from mother to baby. She does this by feeding the baby, or joey, on some of her feces, which contain the bacteria. One of the most typical of Australian sights is a mother koala and her joey perched in a tree fork, munching away. Unfortunately, koalas are not as cuddly as they look. In reality, they are strong, and when confronted by humans, will strike out with sharp claws.

The Australian bush is home to hundreds of bird species. It is a surprise to see parrots flying from tree to tree, as well as clouds of multicolored budgerigars, and lorikeets. Strange, too, are the sounds, the "whip" of the whipbird, and the laughing of the kookaburra. It really does sound like the laugh of a mad person, and it is not surprising how it frightened the early settlers.

BEFORE THE EUROPEANS

Koala bears live on a diet of leaves from eucalyptus or gum trees. Gum trees are very tough, and even able to survive forest fires. Different types have adapted to every extreme of climate in Australia, from the snowy mountains, to the wet, warm tropical areas, or the dry hot plains.

Special, too, are the lyrebirds. These are so-called because the male can spread a great tail of beautiful feathers that looks like a lyre, a harp-like musical instrument. This impresses the female, and he woos her with an unbelievable mimicry of other birds' song. The bowerbird's specialty is an elaborate nest handed down from one generation

15

AUSTRALIA

Caught in the camera's flash, a lyrebird displays his magnificent tail. Lyrebirds live in the forest of eastern Australia. They sing loudly and are excellent mimics.

to the next. Each new male decorates its nest with fronds and flowers and seeds to attract a female.

Marsupials

The trees are home to 22 species of possum that belong to the marsupial family. Marsupials are a special class of the warm-blooded animals called mammals. The marsupial baby grows inside the mother's womb, but unlike foals or human

BEFORE THE EUROPEANS

babies, the marsupial baby is born before it has completely developed and while still very tiny (a third of an inch or so long). This half-embryo, half-baby crawls through the fur on its mother's stomach until it finds a special pouch. Inside, are teats or milk-glands for the baby's nourishment, and there it spends several months finishing its development. In the last weeks of its growth, it may hop out of the pouch for forays into the world outside, and jump back in if danger threatens. Koalas are also marsupials.

Animals of the bush and outback

As the Australian forests receded millions of years ago, some marsupials started to live on the ground. From their branch-hopping ancestry, the wallabies and kangaroos, which are unique to

There are 90 different kinds of kangaroo and wallaby. The largest is the red kangaroo, taller than a man and weighing up to 200 pounds. The smallest is the kangaroo rat which stands only 12 inches tall. Kangaroos can be found all over Australia but they are often thought of as pests by farmers because they compete with sheep for food.

Australia, became land-hoppers.

Also unique to Australia is the emu, the second largest bird in the world after the ostrich. The emu cannot fly, but it can run long distances at speeds of up to 30 miles per hour. It is a good swimmer, too.

There are many reptile species, with 300 different kinds of lizards. Iguanas can grow up to eight feet long. Some of Australia's 110 snake species are poisonous and can kill humans.

Monotremes
Monotremes are unique because they are the only mammals that lay eggs. The only two remaining monotremes are found in Australia, the echidna (or spiny anteater) and the duck-billed platypus.

The platypus is a large furry creature, two feet long, which hunts for food in rivers or creeks. It has a duck-like bill and webbed feet. The young are born in burrows that may stretch for up to 98 feet into the river-bank. The mother can carry them around in her pouch, which has a special watertight seal so that they do not drown.

Water animals
Some people may know about one very dangerous reptile that inhabits northern Queensland from seeing the *Crocodile Dundee* films, but there are plenty of other animals living in Australian waters. Some of the sandy islands surrounding parts of Australia's shores are home to giant turtles. The southern seas, particularly around Tasmania, used to swarm with schools of whales and colonies of seals. Today, seals are still there, but far fewer in numbers, while the

intelligent whales have been hunted close to extinction. Sharks of all sizes are common around Australia. Off the coast of Queensland, the Great Barrier Reef is a coral home for thousands of brilliantly colored fish, including the strange dragon fish which has fronds and fringes, making it look exactly like seaweed.

The first Australians
No one quite knows when the first people arrived in Australia, but it was some time between 40,000 and 100,000 years ago. Quite possibly they migrated from Asia, sailing in primitive canoes the short distances from one island to the next, until they reached New Guinea. The sea level was much lower thousands of years ago, so these first people could have walked from New Guinea to northern Australia. The Aboriginal people living in Australia when the Europeans arrived were descendants of these original inhabitants. The word "aboriginal" actually means "from the beginning."

In parts of Victoria and Tasmania, there is evidence that groups of Aboriginals settled in one place to become farmers. The majority, though, kept to a life on the move. This meant they had few possessions and much of what they had might be for use by everyone. Heavy stones suitable for grinding seeds would be left behind for future use, so that ideas of personal property had little meaning for the Aboriginals.

Trading was important though, with coastal groups exchanging salt for flints made by inland groups, for example. Such trading networks spread across the whole continent. Aboriginal

AUSTRALIA

The Aboriginal people of Australia have one of the longest continuous cultures in existence and ceremonial dances always have been, and still are, important to their lives. From the beginning they were nomads, small bands of people moving across the land, surviving by hunting kangaroos and other animals, and gathering grubs, berries, and nuts.

people learned to live in all parts of Australia, even in the apparently barren deserts. They lived in harmony with the land, because they knew that if they stayed too long in one place or hunted too many animals, they in turn would starve.

Aboriginals did have some effect on the balance of Australian natural life, though. They brought dogs with them, the ancestors of today's dingoes. They brought fire and regularly burned areas of scrub in a controlled way. This helped create larger areas of grasslands suitable for their source of meat, kangaroos, as well as encouraging other edible plant species.

The arrival of Europeans with their own animals such as cows, sheep, and rabbits, would change the face and environment of Australia more than any other single event.

3 Explorers, Convicts, and Settlers

Many people think that Captain Cook was the first European to set foot on Australian shores. They are wrong. There were many before him.

> **Some Early Visitors**
>
> **150 A.D.** Greek geographer Ptolemy wonders if there is a Terra Australis Incognita (Latin for Unknown Land of the South).
>
> **1432** A Chinese fleet lands on what was possibly Australia.
>
> **16th century** Portuguese maps show a coast that may be Australia. Indonesians regularly visit the north coast.
>
> **1606** Portuguese/Dutch navigator Willem Jansz sights and lands on Cape York peninsula. He thinks it is part of New Guinea.
>
> **1616** Dutch sea captain Dirck Hartog nails an inscribed pewter plate to a tree-stump on the western coast to mark his discovery. Other Dutch navigators sight the west, southwest, and northwest coasts.
>
> **1642** Dutch sea captain Abel Tasman explores south coast of Australia, calling the land New Holland. He calls what is now Tasmania, Van Diemen's Land.
>
> **1688** English pirate William Dampier stays three months on the northwest coast of Australia.
>
> **1770** Captain Cook of the British navy, in his ship Endeavour, visits New Zealand and then the Australian east coast.

Although Captain Cook wasn't the first European to set foot on an Australian beach, he did chart the east coast and claimed the land for Great Britain, naming it New South Wales. Sir Joseph Banks, the ship's naturalist, was so excited by the many strange plants growing in one inlet, that he named it Botany Bay.

Criminals and transportation
At that time, life in Britain was a terrible struggle for anyone not born rich. Families of eight or more children, many of whom would die young, were cramped in single dark rooms in old tenement buildings. Children and parents went ragged and barefoot, in complete contrast to professional people and nobility who rode by in carriages, dressed in lace and jewelry.

As a result of these enormous differences, poor people turned to theft and crime to make ends meet. The government in turn used very severe penalties. You could be hanged for stealing bread or a purse. However, the government often reduced sentences from hanging to transportation. This meant sending a convict to do hard labor overseas. It was almost like slavery.

For most of the eighteenth century, transported convicts were sent to North America, but in 1776 America became independent. This posed a great problem for the British government: what to do with the growing numbers of convicts? At first, they were piled into hulks — leaky old warships moored in the Thames River and elsewhere. Then the Home Secretary, Lord Sydney, remembered Captain Cook's report. Australia would be an ideal place for transportation, not only because

EXPLORERS, CONVICTS, AND SETTLERS

the convicts could be "lost" 12,000 miles away, but also because of Britain's trading rivals. Some people thought that France wanted to set up a naval base in Australia. A new colony would make them think twice.

The First Fleet

Accordingly, Captain Arthur Phillip was appointed to lead a first fleet of 11 convict ships. They were tiny sailing boats, smaller than the modern ferries in Sydney Harbor. Into the ships were packed over 750 convicts in chains. With the Marine guards and sailors, nearly 1,500 people set sail from Portsmouth, England, on May 13, 1787. The stormy voyage took eight months and over 40 people died. This was a small number compared to later convict transports, run for profit.

Botany Bay did not turn out to be the paradise Cook and Banks had described, so Phillip sailed north into Port Jackson. On the southern shore he found a good anchorage and named it Sydney Cove, in honor of the Home Secretary. It was January 26, 1788.

Early settlement

Life in the early colony was hard. To begin with, the colonists lived in tents. They had only what they had brought with them or could make. Their cows and sheep wandered off because there were no fences and the first crops failed. This was partly because there were hardly any farmers in the First Fleet, and partly because the seeds they had brought with them were not suited to the climate and soil. For several years the colony nearly starved.

The Aboriginal people watched these feeble attempts at farming and tried to show the settlers how to forage and hunt. In return, the Aboriginals were captured and shot. The Aboriginals had no natural resistance to European diseases; they soon began to get ill, and thousands died. There were possibly a million Aboriginals in 1788. By 1888 there were only 50,000.

As the convicts cleared the bush, and used hand-plows to turn the soil, the Sydney Cove settlement grew inland along the banks of the Parramatta River. Marines and sailors began to set up their own farms because land could be bought very cheaply. Settlers came from Great Britain, first in a trickle, later in a flood.

> Convicts usually served seven years. When they were freed, or emancipated, many stayed in the colony. There they had a chance to become prosperous. The free settlers tried to keep apart from these "Emancipists" and called themselves "Exclusives." Their children were "Sterling Lads and Lasses" named because "Sterling" was the official British coinage. The Emancipist children were "Currency Lads and Lasses," because the early colony's money was an unusual mixture of British and other countries' coins.

Crossing the Blue Mountains

To find enough land, these early settlers had to move farther and farther west of Sydney, until they came up against a natural barrier, the Blue Mountains. Many people looked for a route across, only to find themselves in a dead-end of

EXPLORERS, CONVICTS, AND SETTLERS

steep cliffs, ravines, and impenetrable eucalyptus scrub.

Finally, in 1813, Gregory Blaxland, William Lawson, and William Wentworth were successful in crossing this rough terrain, and found themselves looking out over a vast and apparently uninhabited plain. Not long after, convict chain gangs hacked the hairpin bends of a steep and narrow road through the sandstone, and the settlers' bullock-teams could start to open up the interior. For the settlers, this vast savannah landscape meant wealth. For the Aboriginal people, the settlers' arrival meant disaster.

The early wealth of Australia came from wool. So much so, that the Australian economy was said to "ride on the sheep's back." While the climate made crop-growing unpredictable, flocks of sheep in the thousands could be reared and pastured on vast acreages. In comparison with the average Montana ranch of 2,500 acres, an Australian ranch might contain 12,500 acres.

Of course there were drawbacks. English sheep, bred for a rainy climate, did poorly in Australia. Success only came when merino sheep, which are specially adapted for hot climates, were introduced in the early 1800s. John and Elizabeth Macarthur became famous for breeding suitable varieties.

A clash of beliefs

Convicts, newly arrived in Sydney, would be assigned to settlers, and a common job was to shepherd the vast flocks of sheep. It was a lonely job, and often they would be attacked by Aboriginals. The Aboriginal people had good

AUSTRALIA

Aboriginal people did not divide animals into wild animals and farm animals, so it seemed natural to hunt sheep. These old drawings show that the settlers, who had paid and cared for their sheep, thought differently and often took revenge for sheep killings.

reason for this revenge. The sheep competed for grazing with kangaroos, and so the Aboriginals saw their way of life threatened. Sometimes, they would spear sheep instead. They did not believe it was possible for living things to be owned. Kangaroos could be killed, provided you killed no more than you needed. They saw no reason why sheep should be treated differently.

EXPLORERS, CONVICTS, AND SETTLERS

On the other hand, the British settlers came from a land where all food animals, even birds such as pheasants, belonged to someone. A poacher could be hanged, making a single animal as valuable as a human's life, so the settlers were enraged by any sheep-killing. They took the law into their own hands and started shooting Aboriginals who killed their sheep.

The Aboriginals mounted return attacks, but their spears were no match for guns. Increasingly they were pushed off the land. In Tasmania, the Aboriginals were hunted by soldiers with rifles and rounded up by 1834. On the mainland, Aboriginals had to find occasional work with the European settlers, as trackers of escaped convicts or as highly proficient "cowboys." They could only keep their traditional way of life in remote areas.

A difficult life

Life for the early settlers, and particularly the women, was very hard. In their split-log hovels, they were plagued with flies, mosquitoes, strange insects, and enormous spiders. Some spiders had a bite that could paralyze and even kill. Food spoiled rapidly in the heat, and the nearest store might be hundreds of miles away. Bringing up children was extremely difficult in such conditions, and many died young.

Although sheep brought wealth for a few, early Australia was, in a general way, poor. There were very few brick or stone buildings. Furniture was often homemade. Many of life's necessities had to be imported, with the cost of the sea journey making necessities very expensive. Australia only began to be wealthy when gold was found.

AUSTRALIA

Life in the bush was hard for this family, but by 1890 their lonely wooden slab hut had a corrugated iron roof.

The gold rushes

The first gold discoveries were made in 1851 near Bathurst in New South Wales, and then at Ballarat and Bendigo in Victoria. Thousands of people rushed to the goldfields, not only men but whole families, all digging and panning for the elusive specks that might mean a fortune.

Australia's Labour and Trade Union Movement can be dated to the Gold Rushes. In order to start digging, a "Miner's Right" was needed — written permission from the Colonial Government. At first, this license cost £1.50 each month, about the same as a laborer's weekly wage.

By 1854, gold was becoming scarce, and the license fee, now doubled, seemed totally

EXPLORERS, CONVICTS, AND SETTLERS

unreasonable. At the Eureka diggings on the Ballarat goldfield, a group of miners barricaded themselves in, and burned their licenses. The Governor of Victoria sent in troops, and in the battle of the Eureka Stockade, 30 diggers were killed and 13 arrested; five troopers were killed.

The rebellion had its effect, though, and the fee was soon reduced to £1 per year. In many ways, the Eureka Stockade marked a turning point. Before that time, Australia was first and foremost a penal (punishment) colony ruled by the State Governors. Afterward, Australia was set on the road to democracy, and the concept of one person, one vote. Workers started local trade unions and by the 1890s, because of widespread unemployment, the unions were beginning to make networks nationwide.

At the gold diggings some miners used pans to wash away the dirt and leave the heavy gold specks behind. Wealthier miners could afford a wooden panning machine which did the job more easily and quickly.

29

AUSTRALIA

Bushrangers

Transportation of convicts ended in 1868, but from the start a few prisoners had escaped. Some managed to survive in the bush by hunting, raiding outlying properties, or living with Aboriginal people. These runaways were called bushrangers. With the discovery of gold came a wonderful opportunity. Bushrangers could make a fortune by stealing gold from miners on their way to the banks.

The most famous bushranger of all was Ned Kelly. He and his gang were in a gunfight that resulted in the deaths of three troopers. In some ways they tried to help people. For example, when they robbed the Jerilderie bank, they tore up the deeds of poor settlers' mortgages.

Finally Kelly was captured at Glenrowan, he was taken to Melbourne, tried, and hanged. At only 25 years old he became a legend.

After hunting the Kellys for two years, the police besieged the gang at the inn in Glenrowan. Expecting a shoot-out, the gang had made iron armor for themselves. In the middle of the gunfire, Ned advanced on the police wearing a strange robot-like helmet. He seemed invulnerable, until the police shot his legs below the armor.

30

4 Independent Australia

One hundred years ago, the British still thought of Australia as a group of separate colonies rather than a single nation. Indeed, in 1850 the British Parliament gave each colony the right to establish its own government and make its own laws. Even people living in Australia thought of themselves as colonial British, part of an Empire, rather than as Australians.

More and more, though, this idea of being colonial British was changing. People were coming from countries all over the world, lured by the prospect of cheap land and mineral wealth. Many Australians were native-born. Their home was Australia, not Britain at all.

1788 The colony of New South Wales established, covering the whole eastern half of Australia.
1825 Van Diemen's Land (Tasmania) given separate administration. Brisbane settled.
1829 The colony of Western Australia founded.
1835 Foundation of Melbourne.
1836 Adelaide settled.
1851 Victoria created as a separate colony.
1855 Van Diemen's Land renamed Tasmania.
1856 South Australia created as a separate colony.
1859 Queensland proclaimed a separate colony.
1863 Northern Territory taken over from New South Wales by South Australian administration.

AUSTRALIA

Federation

By the 1890s the feeling of being Australian rather than British was widespread. Politicians, newspapers, and people everywhere began to discuss whether to join the colonies together into one nation — to federate. Federation made most sense for the colonies in the east and south, already closely linked by railroad, river, and sea. The promise of a trans-Australia ("across Australia") rail link was important in persuading the western colony around Perth to agree.

Federation became a reality on January 1, 1901. With it, came a new problem: where to site the Federal Australian Government? Sydney and Melbourne had for a long time rivaled each other in claiming to be Australia's first city. Now they both wanted to be capital. In the end, it was decided that a completely new city would be built. This was Canberra, roughly half way between the rivals.

Federation did not change Australia overnight, and British affairs had a strong influence for many years. Indeed, Australian history since 1901 is about a nation establishing its own identity.

1914 — 1939

When World War I began in 1914, it seemed natural to many people for Australia (and New Zealand) to join in on Great Britain's side. Australia's Prime Minister said the country would fight to "the last man and the last shilling."

The Anzacs, as the Australian and New Zealand Army Corps were called, fought important campaigns, in particular at Gallipoli in Turkey. This was almost a suicide mission. The

INDEPENDENT AUSTRALIA

This photograph is of some troops of the Australian and New Zealand Army Corps or ANZACS, being transported to Gallipoli in 1915. It clearly shows the slouch hats worn by the Anzacs. One side is pinned up so that a rifle can be carried on the shoulder. Anzacs became known as diggers from the cry at Gallipoli, "Dig in!" that was the signal for each soldier to start digging a trench.

Anzacs had to land on a heavily-defended rocky beach. Caught in a hail of machine-gun fire they suffered heavy casualties. After eight months and thousands of dead and wounded, the Army High Command decided to withdraw the Anzacs. In all, 7,818 Australian soldiers had been killed. The Anzacs were then sent to fight in the trenches of France and Belgium, where thousands more died. In total about 60,000 Australians and 17,000 New Zealanders died in World War I. The Anzacs' isolation and heroism led to a belief that with Gallipoli, Australia came of age as a nation.

In the period between the World Wars, Australian history followed a similar pattern to Britain's and the United States'. Automobiles

AUSTRALIA

airplanes, films, radio — all suddenly seemed to come within reach of ordinary people and to offer them a new age of prosperity.

For a few short years after World War I, people lived well. However, prosperity was shortlived. Suddenly, in 1929, Australia found, like other countries, that it could not sell its goods abroad. Bales of wool and mountains of wheat piled up in warehouses. As factories closed or reduced their work forces, workers lost their jobs. This Great Depression, as it was called, was worldwide. Wealthy people in Australia, as elsewhere, lived much as ever, but for poor people and families of the unemployed, life was grim.

1939 onward

When Great Britain went to war with Germany in 1939, Australia again sent troops, leaving Australia almost undefended. Then in 1941,

Japanese planes bombed Darwin, in northern Australia, in February 1942, causing 600 casualties.

34

Japan attacked the American fleet at Pearl Harbor and began conquering countries all around the western rim of the Pacific.

The Japanese reached New Guinea, just north of Australia in March 1942, but this was the turning point of the war. From huge bases in Queensland, Americans and Australians fought a terrible battle in New Guinea, as much against horrific jungle conditions as against the enemy. Finally, after three more years of fighting, Japan (along with Germany and Italy) was defeated.

Pacific awareness
When the United States came to Australia's aid because Britain could not, Australians began to realize that their nearest interests lay in the Pacific. Indeed, when the U.S. fought in Vietnam during the 1960s and 1970s, the Australian government chose at first to send troops in support.

Since the 1950s, Australians have become steadily better off. Today more than ever, Australians see themselves as an independent nation with distinctive Australian values. This sense of independence is not only felt by politicians, it can be seen in the flourishing of Australian arts since the 1960s.

The Arts today
Australian novelists such as Patrick White, Thomas Keneally, Peter Carey, Frank Moorhouse, and Elizabeth Jolley have become internationally recognized. Australian filmmakers have made new and original films like *Breaker Morant* and *Picnic at Hanging Rock*, as well as popular successes such as the *Mad Max* and

AUSTRALIA

Australia's most famous building, the Sydney Opera House, was designed by Danish architect, Joern Utzon. It was opened to the public by Queen Elizabeth II in 1973.

Crocodile Dundee films. For a long time, Australian television has bought soap operas from Britain and the United States, but with *Neighbours* it is now returning the compliment. Australian pop singers like Kylie Minogue and such groups as *INXS, Midnight Oil,* and *Mental As Anything* have become famous worldwide.

The Aboriginal people, too, are finding ways of making their voice heard through the arts. Jack Davis's plays have been performed internationally. Oodgeroo Noonuccal (Kath Walker) has published novels and poetry about Aboriginal experiences. In 1987 the first Black Playwright's Conference was held in Canberra to promote Aboriginal writing. Groups such as *Coloured Stone* and the *Warumpi Band* are creating modern music using traditional instruments.

For a long time during the country's expansion, Australians had little time for the arts. Now one of the strongest visual symbols of Australia is the daring architecture of Sydney's Opera House.

5 Bullocks, Camels, and Qantas

In any land, but particularly in a vast land like Australia, people need to get themselves and their goods easily from one place to another. Good communications and transportation mean trade can increase and people prosper.

Dreaming paths and roads
When the first settlers landed there were no roads. What they could not see were tracks known very well to the Aboriginal people. These were trade routes spreading across the whole continent. The Aboriginals exchanged pointed stones from the Kimberleys, boomerangs from the Gulf of Carpentaria, red ochre for body paint from the Flinders Ranges. All these goods were handed on in dancing ceremonies from one tribe to another, even across the vast inland deserts. The exchange paths were called the Dreaming Tracks, and as their name suggests, were much more than trading routes. (See Chapter 10.)

Intent on making fortunes, the early settlers needed roads to move supplies inland and to send back wagon loads of wool bales, as well as sheep to the markets and slaughterhouses. Many of today's asphalt highways are laid over macadam roadbeds whose stones were first broken up and hammered into place by chaingangs.

Goods moved along the early roads in wagons pulled by bullock teams. The long slow journeys added to the price of goods by the time they

AUSTRALIA

In the days before the invention of the car, transportation was a major problem in Australia. Everything had to be transported inland from the large cities and ports near the coast. Large teams of oxen were used to pull huge cartloads of goods.

reached settlers far inland. This was in addition to the cost of shipping goods from Britain. Ordinary household items, furniture, and hardware like door-latches, were scarce and expensive until well into the nineteenth century and it was a long time before such items were made in quantity in Australia. Eventually motor transportation arrived and, of course, brought immense changes. Today a common sight is a huge road-train with a truck pulling two or even three trailers loaded with merchandise.

River transportation

In developing countries, rivers are an important transportation alternative to roads. In Australia, the scarcity of the rivers slowed down the spread of settlers. However, the huge Murray-Darling river system was developed to provide 3,410 miles of navigable waterway.

BULLOCKS, CAMELS, AND QANTAS

In the 1850s paddlewheel steamers began a regular service from the mouth of the Murray to settlements hundreds of miles inland. The whole region became linked to the clipper-ship port of Victor Harbor. Settlers now could export wool in vast quantities. The result was that loading docks and shipwrights' yards sprang up all along the river. Enormous trunks of red gum trees were floated from the top of the Murray River downstream to be sawn and shaped into boats. Around these workplaces, towns grew up and many, such as Echuca, became important inland ports.

The rivers had a drawback. Their great loops doubled distances and because of Australia's intermittent rainfall, they were navigable for only eight months of the year. Soon they were overtaken by railroads.

Railroads

The first Australian railroad was manpowered by convicts and ran across the Tasman peninsula. The second was a horse tramway connecting Goolwa at the mouth of the Murray River, with Port Elliot and Victor Harbor. The very first steam train ran 2.5 miles from Melbourne to Sandridge on September 12, 1854.

Slowly in the 1860s and 1870s, railroads spread out from the main cities. At first, the plan was to follow the Irish example, with a gauge, or distance between the rails, of 5 feet 3 inches. Melbourne's railroad was built to this standard and Adelaide's, too. Then Sydney's railroad was built to the British standard of 4 feet 8$^1/_2$ inches. But Queensland decided there would not be

AUSTRALIA

The Indian Pacific is like a traveling hotel, with its own chef creating elaborate meals. There's even a piano for entertainment, and you can wake at dawn in your sleeping berth to see kangaroos bounding along beside the train.

enough traffic for a full-size railroad and chose the narrow 3 feet 6 inches gauge.

Had the colonies stayed completely separate, the gauge differences might not have mattered. However, as settlers spread out from the seaports, the railroads followed. Eventually they met. Where they did meet, the townships that grew up became known as "break-of-gauge" towns. Traveling from Sydney to Melbourne for example, all freight as well as passengers had to cross the platform at Albury to a different gauge train. The transfer was a nuisance, and added to the cost of transporting goods.

BULLOCKS, CAMELS, AND QANTAS

Across Australia
In the 1900s, Western Australia seemed very remote from the eastern states, and a trans-Australia railway was proposed. The missing section was between Kalgoorlie and Port Augusta, a distance of 1,060 miles, and this was finally completed in 1917 after nine years' work. Even so, the gauge-breaks meant passengers traveled on four different trains between Perth and Adelaide.

Today a single train makes the three-day run, which is one of the world's great train journeys and includes the longest stretch of straight railway line, 295 miles across the Nullarbor Plain.

It wasn't until the 1960s that the main lines were standardized and the break-of-gauge problem was rectified. Nevertheless, there are still many narrow gauge railways, particularly the sugarcane lines in Queensland. The importance of bulk ore shipments and the cost of air tickets means that railroads are still an important means of transportation both for freight and people.

Explorers
Roads, rivers, and railroads could not solve all of Australia's early communications problems. The big barrier was the desert in the center of Australia. To cope with conditions around the edges, camels and their drivers were brought from Afghanistan, and are still used today. It was the center of Australia that held fascination for the early explorers.

Edward Eyre and Charles Sturt searched deep inland for new grazing pasture, but it was Robert Burke and William Wills who set off in 1860 on an expedition to cross the continent from south to north for the first time. Their six months' endurance in the hot central deserts and the wet northern tropics was rewarded when they finally reached the mangrove swamps on the Gulf of Carpentaria. Sadly the return journey ended in tragedy when the explorers reached their base camp. Digging up a buried message, at a spot now called the Dig Tree, they learned they had missed a relief party by a few hours. Buried supplies kept them going a while longer, but weak and ill, both Burke and Wills died in the bush.

Telegraph and radio
Surprisingly, it was only a few years later that a telegraph line was laid across the same central deserts to link Adelaide with Darwin. There, in 1872, it picked up the line stretching across Asia and Europe to London. In less than 100 years the time taken to send a message from London to Sydney and receive a reply, had been reduced from a year (by sailing ship) to seconds.

From the 1920s on, radio communication has taken over from the telegraph. At first, distant homesteads could buy a two-way radio powered by a pedal generator. Now station managers can use CB-type radios to keep in touch with their stockmen. Solar energy has become a new way of powering distant telephone connections.

By air and sea
One of the biggest changes came with the development of commercial aircraft in the 1920s and 1930s. Suddenly, the state capitals shrank from being days away from each other to only a

BULLOCKS, CAMELS, AND QANTAS

few hours. At the same time, the lack of roads in the outback became much less important. A large grass field could easily become a simple airstrip for a light aircraft.

After World War II, aircraft companies grew and merged. The major internal airlines are Ansett and Australian Airlines, while Qantas has grown to be Australia's international airline. Qantas is a company that thinks big: it flies only jumbo jets.

With jumbo jets go jumbo-sized ore-carriers. These immense ships sail vast quantities of minerals from Australia as raw minerals for the factories of industrialized countries such as Japan and China. One bulk ore freighter at 200,000 tons weighs as much as two aircraft carriers put together.

Distances are so great in Australia that planes of all sizes are used for transporting both people and goods. Many farmers use two-seater planes to herd their sheep but these huge jumbo jets are used by Qantas for flying around the world.

43

AUSTRALIA

6   A Living From the Land

As much as 64 percent of Australia's land is used for agriculture but most of this is marginal grazing country of little value. Australia is the world's largest exporter of beef, veal, lamb, and live sheep. About one-quarter of the world's wool comes from Australia. Other major crops include wheat, barley, rice, oats, sugar, cotton, and fruit.

Farming in the outback
The early settlers discovered that inland, Australia's thin vegetation meant huge areas were needed to support profitable numbers of sheep and cattle. Today, farms that are over half a million acres in size are common. Australians call such huge farms sheep or cattle stations. Large stations with windpumps and dams to provide water may support 15,000 sheep in a good year or in a dry season, perhaps 5,000 can still be raised. The world's largest cattle station, 11,580 square miles, is Strangeray Springs, South Australia. This station alone is nearly the size of Belgium.

A cattle station is run by the owner or manager, and a handful of stockmen, or cowboys. Originally, horses were used for mustering, or rounding up, the stock, but motorbikes and trucks are increasingly common. At sheep shearing time, a team of professional shearers will work in a large shearing shed for several weeks before moving on to the next station. Running a station is a hard, 24 hour a day job, and because most stations are far from towns of any size, everyone must be self-sufficient, learning

A LIVING FROM THE LAND

Sheep and cattle stations in the outback are very far apart, almost hidden in a wild and empty landscape. This farm or "station" is in the Palmer Valley, 100 miles south of Alice Springs in the Northern Territory. This station has 2,048 square miles of land!

first-aid as well as how to repair utility trucks and diesel generators.

Children growing up on outback stations have to learn to be equally self-sufficient. They can usually drive motorbikes and trucks before they are ten years old, and go out mustering or rabbit-shooting along with the adults. Children can be lonely because their nearest friend may live more than 100 miles away.

School of the air

In the outback, going to school is often replaced by School of the Air. This is an idea unique to Australia. School of the Air is a form of distance learning where the teacher talks over the radio to a "class" of four or five children, each in their own

AUSTRALIA

There are 12 Schools of the Air broadcasting to children too far from ordinary schools to attend. On average there are 100 pupils aged from four to twelve being taught by each school.

schoolroom on their station. The radio sets are two-way, so children can press the "transmit" key and talk to their teacher. Usually one of the parents continues where School of the Air leaves off. Written work is mailed to the far-away teaching center, checked by the teacher and returned. Children and teachers get to know each other each year in special summer camps.

Flying doctors

If someone is very ill, or badly injured, help can be asked for over the radio-telephone. Each station has a medical kit with numbered medicines, and a doctor or nurse can advise over the air which is the best medication. If that is not enough, the Flying Doctor Service can be called in. A light

A LIVING FROM THE LAND

plane or helicopter with a doctor and assistant lands on the nearest flat ground, the patient is put into the aircraft on a stretcher, and a hour or two later may be in the operating room of a hospital hundreds of miles away. It's a very Australian way of adapting to life in a huge, sparsely-populated country.

Aboriginals and the outback

To Europeans, the outback can seem a hostile place. To Aboriginals, who see the land as their Mother, it is a source of food and life. While the men have always gone tracking and hunting,

This Aboriginal woman has collected plants, insects, and grubs for food, and put them in a woven mesh bag. She is also carrying small palms slung over her digging stick.

AUSTRALIA

more regular food has come from foraging by the women. At an early age, they learn where to dig for roots and tubers and how to strip bark from trees to reveal edible insects. An important (and nutritionally balanced) food is the witchetty grub, about the size of a large prawn.

Living a nomadic life, outback Aboriginals learn how to weave temporary shelters called *mia-mias* from branches and leaves. Aboriginals know how to be at home in the desert and semidesert of the interior. Other Australians are learning to value the Aboriginal's knowledge of the land.

New plants and animals

Settlers brought rabbits with them for food, but without natural enemies, the rabbits bred and bred, until they became a plague, a "gray tide." They were so plentiful that 22 million frozen rabbits were exported by 1906, earning more than beef exports. Rabbits destroyed large areas of pastureland and people tried unsuccessfully to fence them out. It was only when they were deliberately infected with the terrible disease myxamatosis that the rabbit population was kept in check.

Similar problems occurred with the prickly pear cactus which spread rampantly until modern weed killers were able to control it. In Queensland, cane toads were introduced to kill sugarcane pests, but with nothing to prey on them, became pests themselves.

Sadly, where forests have been cleared, the land often proves unsuitable for agriculture and remains barren. In the outback, overstocking with sheep can destroy the thin vegetation. By

The waratah is a striking native Australian flower, but to the early settlers, Australia seemed lacking in beauty and they introduced many pretty flowering shrubs and trees such as frangipani, hibiscus, and bougainvillea.

A LIVING FROM THE LAND

contrast, traditional Aboriginal lifestyles were in harmony with the land. The Australian lesson is that modern agriculture can all too easily upset the ecological balance.

Crops

Australia's principal crop is wheat. It is the third largest wheat exporting country after the United States and Canada. Wheat is grown in a belt of land stretching southeast from Perth, and in a crescent from Adelaide through Victoria and New South Wales to Brisbane. However, Australian agriculture is much more than sheep and wheat.

The tropical climate of coastal Queensland is ideal for growing sugarcane. Narrow-gauge railroads take huge loads of canes to the sugar

Burning the sugar crop cleans off all the leaves ready for cutting the cane, and drives out animals and snakes that may attack the cutters.

AUSTRALIA

Some areas, such as the Barossa valley in South Australia have been producing good wine for well over 100 years since German settlers brought their traditional methods with them. South Australia is still the principal wine-growing area, but wine is also made around Perth as well as in Victoria and New South Wales.

processing plants. After the harvest, the woody undergrowth of the canes is burned off in spectacular, controlled fires. In the nineteenth century Torres Strait and Pacific islanders were forcibly brought onto the mainland to work on the plantations. The *Kanakas*, as they were called, were treated like slaves.

Queensland is also the home of delicious Macadamia nuts — a treat rare outside Australia. Macadamias are grown commercially in Hawaii, but it is only recently that they have begun to be farmed in the country they come from.

Fruit
On the other hand, Tasmania's climate is quite cool, with a heavy dose of rain, 40-80 inches per

A LIVING FROM THE LAND

year. Crops, such as hops and apples grow so well that people call it "The Apple Isle."

Soft fruit needs water, and it is not surprising that Australia's main areas for citrus fruits and stone fruits — peaches, plums, and apricots — are in Riverina and along the Murray River where irrigation is good. Nearby canning factories mean that much of the fruit can be exported.

These areas are also important for dried fruit such as raisins and sultanas. Australia is also becoming known for the quality of its wines.

Cattle

Dairy farming has become important in the temperate areas, mainly in southern Victoria and the eastern New South Wales. On the large outback stations, however, cattle are raised for beef. Steak is cheap, and Australians eat a lot of it; they also export it.

7 Opals, Gold, and Iron Mountains

The discovery of gold near Bathurst alerted Australians to the presence of valuable minerals. If these could be dug out and sold overseas, Australia could become a rich country. For years, prospectors roamed inland, hoping to strike other goldfields. They were usually unlucky, but sometimes found valuable deposits of other minerals.

Coober Pedy
Opals are beautiful gems, with rainbow colors flecking a cloudy or blue background. One of the famous opal fields is at Coober Pedy in South Australia. It was originally discovered in 1915 by prospectors searching unsuccessfully for gold. Around £750 worth of opals were mined in 1916, and this increased rapidly to £24,000 worth in 1920. Today it is a multimillion dollar industry and tourists flock to Coober Pedy.

Apart from buying opals, people come to see the unusual lifestyle of the miners. Coober Pedy is very hot and dry, with temperatures reaching 113°F in summer, and dropping to 39°F during winter. To avoid these extremes, the first miners made homes by tunneling into the soft rock. Now Coober Pedy is a warren of underground dwellings, most of them furnished with kitchen appliances, carpets, and furniture just like any other home. There is even an underground hotel. It's a good way to live, because temperatures inside the dugouts remain a steady 70° — 79°F. It

OPALS, GOLD, AND IRON MOUNTAINS

You might think this was some special new architecture until you realize this room is cut out of the rock, as is the rest of this house in Coober Pedy. The rock keeps the house cool in the hot summers.

is from these "burrows" that the township gets its name, from the Aboriginal *kupa pitti* meaning "white man in a hole."

Other minerals

After the gold rushes of the 1850s, gold continued to be the most important of Australia's exports with major new finds in Western Australia and Queensland. Copper and tin were mined from the 1840s, while in 1883, lead and silver were discovered at Broken Hill in western New South Wales. Copper, silver, and lead were also mined in western Tasmania from the 1880s. By the 1930s Mount Isa in Queensland had become an important source of lead and copper.

The 1950s and 1960s saw the discovery of huge

Aboriginal people observing the Ranger uranium mine that is being dug in their ancestral land. Many areas of land that the Aboriginal people hold as sacred are very rich in valuable minerals.

deposits of iron ore in the Pilbara, Western Australia, and bauxite (aluminum ore) near Perth and in Arnhem Land in the Northern Territory and Cape York in Queensland. Australia is now the world's largest producer of bauxite and alumina which is concentrated aluminum ore.

Uranium is an important resource because there are so few worthwhile deposits in the world. Uranium is a radioactive metal. It is a source of atomic energy and is used in nuclear power stations to help produce electricity. It can also be used to make nuclear weapons. There are uranium mines in the Northern Territory and at Roxby Downs in South Australia. Perhaps sensibly, Australia's policy is to have no nuclear power stations of its own.

One of the main uranium mines, Jabiru, is on Aboriginal land. In fact many mining sites are in areas that are sacred to Aboriginal people. There have been some cases where mining companies have negotiated rights with Aboriginals, but these are few.

Newman

Newman in Western Australia was created in the middle of nowhere like Coober Pedy, and also serves a mine. Unlike Coober Pedy, Newman didn't "just grow," it was planned from the start by the Mount Newman Mining Company.

Mount Newman is in the Pilbara, in the northwest of Western Australia, and around it the company leases 300 square miles of land rich in high quality iron ore. The prize orebody, as geologists call it, is Mount Whaleback, which is almost literally a mountain of iron. The company is digging out and selling this mountain of iron ore. Crushers reduce it to fist-sized lumps. Then it is loaded onto trains, ready to transport the iron ore down a specially laid single-line railroad track to Port Hedland 265 miles away. Each train is one and a quarter miles long, hauled by three 3,500 horsepower diesel-electric locomotives. The 180 cars (wagons) carry about 18,000 tons of ore.

To work such a mine, thousands of people are needed, and at the start, there was only bare land for hundreds of miles. Now 6,000 people live in Newman, and the shift pattern of working 24 hours a day means that people often lead topsy-turvy lives with sports, or barbecues through the night.

AUSTRALIA

Everything about Newman is huge. Massive earth movers on caterpillar tracks scoop out the mountainside on a series of levels. Each earth mover is as tall as a two-story house, and the bucket scoops out 50 tons at a single bite. (A small family car weights about a ton.)

Tons of ore

Mining started at Mount Whaleback in 1969 and in 1985 the billionth ton of material had been dug out, of which over 400 million tons was iron ore for shipment. Eventually, the mountain will not only be leveled, but dug deep down to make a lake. Geologists estimate that there are 1.5 billion tons of ore in Mount Whaleback. When that is exhausted, there are other orebodies to be dug out nearby. Some time in the future the iron ore will run out and the reason for the township will disappear. Newman engineers expect to landscape the site, perhaps creating lakes and a resort complex in the barren Pilbara.

At Port Hedland the ore is stockpiled for loading onto some of the world's largest bulk

OPALS, GOLD, AND IRON MOUNTAINS

carrier ships. The ore is made into steel and used to manufacture cars.

Coal and other power
As countries industrialize, they need more and more power. Like the United States and Britain, Australia is lucky to have plenty of coal. Indeed coal was mined in the Hunter Valley north of Sydney in the 1790s using convict labor. From these early beginnings, a huge coal industry grew up in New South Wales, with Newcastle (named for its similarity to the English city) as its port.

In the 1980s, 60 million tons of black steam coal were being mined each year in New South Wales. Another 45 million tons came from mines around Rockhampton in Queensland. Brown coal is mined at Yallourn to fuel Victoria's power stations.

Today oil and gas from the Bass Strait, Queensland, and the North West Shelf, together with smaller fields, supply half of Australia's energy needs.

The Snowy Mountains
Australia has few high mountains so there are not many hydroelectric power projects, for they rely on the energy created by rivers flowing down hill. The best known power plant is the Snowy Mountains Project, begun in 1949 and now generating 4,000 megawatts. It had two main functions: to provide electricity, and improve irrigation. It did this with a series of massive dams and, incredibly, by diverting a river through a mountain. In this way, water from the flood-prone Snowy River could be diverted into the Murray

and Murrumbidgee Rivers, improving irrigation in the important fruit-growing areas. This ambitious project took until 1972 to complete.

The Snowy Mountains Project has not been without drawbacks. Water from irrigation dissolves salt trapped in the soil and carries it back into the Murray River. Lower down the river, the now salty water is used for more irrigation. The water has become so salty though that it is killing plants. In a few years, the river may be useless.

Modern commerce

The last 50 years has seen Australia change from a mainly rural agricultural economy to one that is mixed. It is now one of the world's major producers of minerals, and they are as important to Australia's overseas trade as wool and beef. Australia has developed its own industries, in particular food processing, which accounts for nearly a quarter of all manufacturing output. Like many countries, though, output has hardly grown during the 1970s and 1980s and Australia still relies heavily on imported goods, half of them from the United States and Japan.

Europe used to be Australia's main export market, but now it is Asia. In 1954, 36 percent of Australia's exports went to Great Britain. By 1980, this had dropped to five percent.

Industrialization has enabled businessmen such as Rupert Murdoch and Kerry Packer to make fortunes and become international investors. Rupert Murdoch is particularly well-known outside Australia for his newspaper and communications empire, which includes companies in the United States, Britain, and Canada.

8 Cities

Australians are city dwellers. This does not mean the tightly packed housing that Europeans are used to. Most Australians want their own home on their own piece of ground, and so cities spread for many miles. Sydney's suburbs stretch 25 miles inland.

Sydney, capital of New South Wales
Water and light are Sydney's most noticeable features. From The Rocks area, the huge Harbour Bridge arches across to the North Shore. At nearby Circular Quay, ferries take commuters and tourists to the suburbs and beaches along the water's edge. Brilliant sunshine, sparkling water, and people in bright clothing all give Sydney's center a resort atmosphere.

The Rocks are where the first convicts made their home in 1788, huddled together for safety and scared of the weird bush noises. Traffic now pounds the streets, but some of Australia's oldest buildings are here, turned into tourist attractions.

The main commercial center has grown up just to the south of The Rocks. Its high-rise buildings cluster around the soaring Centrepoint Tower. Large areas of central Sydney are being redeveloped with new underground rail links and submerged freeways.

Farther away, suburbs such as Paddington have close-packed row houses built by nineteenth-century immigrants in imitation of London streets. The imitation is not complete — the verandas and gum trees are an instant give-away.

AUSTRALIA

This is an old inner city area of Sydney known as Paddington. The district became very run down, but in recent years people have begun to appreciate the attractive architecture of the houses and many are being restored.

King's Cross is a seedy suburb where tourists and sailors go for nightlife. Sometimes it can be a dangerous area. Even farther away, places named by homesick British immigrants give way to suburbs with Aboriginal names such as Turramurra and Woollahra.

Many residents of Sydney arrange their jobs to start and finish early so they get an afternoon in the sun. The ferry to the Heads, the entrance to Sydney harbor, passes beach after beach of sunbathers and surfers. After half an hour, the ferry reaches the beach suburb of Manly, so-named by Captain Phillip, the commander of the First Fleet, who was impressed by the manly qualities of the Aboriginals he met there.

You can still visit Botany Bay, but the many

CITIES

Melbourne at night is brightly lit and lively. It is the capital of Victoria and a thriving commercial center, with a population of nearly three million. It is the only city in Australia that still has trolleys, a popular means of transportation.

varieties of trees and shrubs that gave it its name have long since disappeared under the concrete of Sydney's main commercial port.

Melbourne, capital of Victoria

Where Sydney has slightly more than three million inhabitants, Melbourne has slightly less. It is less dramatically situated than Sydney, and the wealth brought to Melbourne in the gold

61

rushes stayed, in the form of solid prosperous-looking stone buildings, many of which still stand. This rather old-fashioned feel is strengthened by the green and yellow trolleys that have become a symbol of Melbourne.

Melbourne has its high-rise center, but it's also a city of parks. The winding Yarra River helps create a sense of tranquillity and in South Yarra, the Royal Botanic Gardens have groves of unusual plants. At the Victorian Arts Center is a concert hall, and theaters for opera, ballet, and drama. Not far away is Melbourne Cricket Ground, seating 110,000, home of the 1956 Olympic Games, and of many famous cricket matches. The Cricket Ground is also where the finals of Australian Rules football are held. Melbourne is the only city in the world to have a public holiday for a horse race. The Melbourne Cup, with a prize of about $250,000 is held on the first Tuesday in November. All of Melbourne seems to go, everyone dressed up for the occasion.

Melbourne is renowned for its suddenly changing weather. Cold winds blowing in from the Antarctic can cause temperatures more like New England than Australia. If the wind changes, the temperature can soar in an hour to 86°F.

Canberra, capital of Australia
It is almost possible to drive around Canberra without realizing you are in a city. This is because its houses and stores are designed around pedestrian malls and because it's a city of trees and lakes. Canberra is a planned city, designed to be the administrative center of Federal Australia. Set in the center of the garden suburbs are

massive modern buildings, the National Library, The National Gallery, The High Court, and the new Parliament House. From Parliament House, there is a wide avenue vista stretching up Anzac Parade to the Australian War Memorial about a mile and a quarter away.

Brisbane, capital of Queensland
Like Sydney, Brisbane is a city on the waterfront, but massive high-rise buildings in the center have replaced many smaller stores and offices. It is the most American of all the Australian cities.

As you drive out from the center, the broad Brisbane River creates an impressive sight with its five bridges, each different in design. The high-rise gives way to traditional Queensland-style buildings. Famous among them is the Breakfast Creek Hotel (usually abbreviated to Brekkie Creek!) built on the spot where John Oxley, the British government's Surveyor General, breakfasted in 1824 as he decided this would be the site for a new convict settlement.

Brisbane enjoys subtropical weather, and it is not surprising that the sandy beaches of the Sunshine Coast are a tourist attraction. The beaches spread well over 62 miles north, while to the south, Surfers Paradise is the center of the Gold Coast. In 1988, Brisbane was host to Expo 88, a major trade and cultural exhibition on the theme of Leisure in the Age of Industry.

Adelaide, capital of South Australia
Named after King William IV's wife, Adelaide is an excellent example of early town planning, comparable with Washington, D.C. or Edinburgh

AUSTRALIA

in Scotland. Its main street is an impressive 130 feet across. Adelaide has little local timber, so there is a higher proportion of brick and stone buildings there than in any other Australian city.

Adelaide has become famous for promoting the arts, and has built a special Festival Center for a biennial Festival of the Arts, which lasts for three weeks. By contrast, Adelaide is also host to the Australian Formula One Grand Prix car race.

Perth, capital of Western Australia

Perth is a remote city, almost four hours flying time and three time zones from the cities of the east coast. Perth used to be a sleepy provincial city, with fine weather similar to, but drier than Sydney's. Some of the unhurried atmosphere remains, but the immense mineral wealth discovered recently in Western Australia has turned Perth into an important commercial center.

It is situated on the Swan River, so-called

Perth is the largest city in Western Australia, of which it is the capital, commercial, and cultural center. The climate is excellent, and the city is steadily expanding.

because of its large number of black swans which have become a symbol for Western Australia. Perth's port is Fremantle, on the mouth of the Swan River.

In 1983 Perth's Alan Bond won the America's Cup yachting trophy, so the city hosted the 1987 race bringing much commercial interest and new tourism to the city. Sadly for Australia, the United States won the cup back in 1987.

Hobart, capital of Tasmania

Australia's second oldest city still has many early stone buildings to remind visitors of the convict system. Indeed Hobart is one of the most English of Australia's cities, with one of the coolest climates. The city is overlooked by Mount Wellington, snowcapped in winter.

The city is built on the banks of the Derwent River, and the shores are linked by the wide, hump-backed Tasman Bridge.

Darwin, administrative capital of the Northern Territory

In contrast to Hobart, Darwin is one of Australia's newest cities, having been rebuilt after Cyclone Tracy flattened it on Christmas Day 1974. It's a tropical city, oppressively humid much of the time and its citizens need their swimming pools more than most Australians.

Darwin is the principal township in the Northern Territory, which is not a separate state, but administered by South Australia. Darwin's closeness to Asia makes it an important base for Australia's defense communications. There is a major military air base located in Darwin.

AUSTRALIA

9 Australians

Australians live a strange mix of lifestyle that is basically British, yet adapted to a hot climate. Clothing and furniture are much the same as in Britain, but houses, the way towns are laid out, and people's use of their spare time are distinctively Australian.

Towns and houses

Off the main streets of a typical small town, the houses have wide verandas as a means of creating drafts and keeping cool. Traditional Australian houses, both in the bush and in cities, had a center hallway with a front and back door usually left open, to let air flow through. In Queensland,

There is no mistaking typical small towns like Braidwood in New South Wales. There is one wide main street, and the shops and buildings are made of clapboard. The footpaths are often roofed over to create shade. Like many Australians, these people strap their surfboards on the car roof and head for the beach on the weekend.

AUSTRALIANS

houses were built on stilts that both made it easier to control ants and termites, and provided more ventilation. The area left open underneath the building became a useful shady work and play space.

As people grew richer in the late nineteenth century, houses were built on very similar lines to large Victorian houses in Britain, with the big difference that they were surrounded by verandas on the ground and first floors. Sometimes the veranda railings were made of beautiful cast-iron lacework.

Homes today still have verandas, but inside they are often open plan, with the living room, dining room, and kitchen all open to each other. Inside, furniture and furnishings are like those you would find inside modern American and

Verandas provide a cool shady place to relax, as well as preventing direct sunlight from entering the rooms. Veranda living is an important part of Australian life, and many families make their verandas comfortable with cane easy chairs and potted plants.

AUSTRALIA

British homes, but you may still find curious old-style furniture like the squatter's chair, designed so that you can sit back and let a draft circulate around your legs and arms. Many people have a swimming pool, and a patio for barbecues.

Language

Films and television have made the sound of Australian English somewhat familiar, although real Australians rarely speak with such a broad accent. It's not hard to understand Australians, but sometimes their words and phrases are unexpectedly different.

Multicultural Australia

Increasingly people from countries other than Britain have arrived in Australia. Chinese came to

Masked figures in the Chinese New Year celebrations in Sydney.

AUSTRALIANS

Oz-Pom Dictionary

arvo	afternoon
barbie	barbecue
beaut	really good
bludger	someone who tries to get out of doing their share of work
Brissie	Brisbane
chook	chicken
Chrissie	Christmas
dobb someone in	tell tales about someone
fair dinkum	genuine
digger	Australian soldier
esky	picnic box to keep things cool
great galah	stupid idiot
milk bar	corner shop selling a bit of everything
mozzie	mosquito
no worries	it will be all right
ocker	truly Australian (once an insult now used patriotically)
paddock	field
pav = pavlova	cream-filled meringue
pressie	present
rellies	relatives
skite	show-off, brag
stickybeak	someone who is very nosey
strine	the accent and vocabulary peculiar to Australia
swaggie/swagman	a wanderer or traveling bush worker who sleeps in the open
tucker	food
ute	utility truck
vegemite	Australian yeast extract
yabbies	edible crayfish, living in dams and nibbling swimmers' toes

work in the goldfields in the 1850s, and they were followed by Germans, many of whom settled around Adelaide.

After World War II, many Australians wanted immigration to Australia to increase. They felt very strongly that a larger population was needed to help with Australia's defense in case there was ever another war. Between 1946 and 1965 around 2.5 million immigrants arrived. Most were on assisted passage programs where they paid a very small fare and the Australian government paid the rest. Half of the new arrivals were British but huge numbers also came from Italy and Greece. Melbourne is now said to be the second largest Greek city in the world after Athens. More recently, large numbers of Vietnamese escaping from the war there (the "boat people") have settled in Australia. Large numbers of people also now migrate to Australia from other Asian and Pacific countries.

Immigrants brought their own traditions with them. Many still celebrate their festivals just as if they were in their home country. Their range of foods and styles of cooking have affected the way all Australians eat. There are Thai restaurants alongside traditional British fish and chip shops, and fruit salad is as likely to include lichees and mangoes as apples and oranges. These influences all make for a very mixed and colorful society.

For newcomers, one of the important moments is when they become naturalized Australians. There is a special ceremony in which they swear allegiance to Australia before being handed the important papers that say they are now full-fledged Australians.

AUSTRALIANS

Anthem and emblem

The national anthem is not, as many people outside Australia think, *Waltzing Matilda*. In fact, it is the much less widely known *Advance Australia Fair*. *Waltzing Matilda* was composed by a well-known folk-singer, Banjo Patterson, in 1895.

Government

Federation created a three-tier system of government in Australia; local, state, and federal. Australians vote for representatives at all three levels. Secret ballots (where no one knows who you vote for) were an Australian idea used first in Victoria and South Australia in 1856.

There are about 900 local government bodies. Local government takes care of garbage collection, water supplies and sewerage, as well as libraries and swimming pools.

Each state has its own government, taking care of such necessities as education, health, transportation, and police.

The Federal tier of government makes laws covering the whole of Australia. It also has Federal Departments with particular responsibilities, such as Defense, Employment and Industrial Relations, Foreign Affairs, Immigration, and Aboriginal Affairs. Similar to the United States, there are two levels of Federal Government: the House of Representatives (Lower House), and the Senate (Upper House). The nearest British equivalents are the House of Commons and House of Lords. Australia is more like Britain in having a Prime Minister and other Ministers who come from the party with a majority in the Lower House. There is no

AUSTRALIA

president, and Australia, which is a member of the Commonwealth, recognizes Britain's queen as Queen of Australia. The queen appoints a governor-general to represent her at federal level and a governor for each State.

The main parties are Labor led by Bob Hawke, (in power in 1988) and the Liberal and National Parties. These two formed a coalition to govern Australia between 1976 and 1983. The Australian Democrats form a much smaller party.

Aboriginal people rally around their black, red, and yellow flag. Black for the people, red for blood and the color of Australian soil, and yellow for the sun.

Aboriginals and land rights

After 200 years of harsh treatment, most Aboriginal people feel they are outsiders in their own country. In the last two decades, there has been a strong Aboriginal Land Rights movement with the aim of regaining some of the ancient tribal territories. Not unreasonably, Aboriginal people feel that they should have a share of the land and their message has been eloquently stated by people such as Robert Bropho, spokesperson for a group of Aboriginals in the Swan Valley near Perth.

The Land Rights campaign has had some success in a country where many people are strongly prejudiced against Aboriginals. Some areas have been established solely for Aboriginal use. Aboriginal people were overjoyed when Ayers Rock was returned to them, and its original name Uluru was officially recognized.

Australia and nuclear weapons
There are other protest movements in Australia, and one of them is People for Nuclear Disarmament. PND is concerned about Australia's current involvement in the nuclear arms race. PND also alerts people to the results of earlier weapons testing, when Britain was allowed to explode nuclear weapons in the Maralinga Desert ignoring the Aboriginal people who were there. Huge areas of the desert are still contaminated and fenced off and many Aboriginal people are still suffering.

AUSTRALIA

10   The Sky Is Our Church

Australians worship the sun. They're less concerned with worshiping in a church. Nevertheless, Australia is basically a Christian society but, as might be expected, the outdoor lifestyle affects the way services take place. Many are held outdoors, and it's common for weddings to be held in the open air, often in gardens. Many churches have wall sections that can be opened.

Christianity
When the colony was founded, early worship followed the Church of England pattern but other Protestant churches were soon established. The many Irish coming to the colony, followed by Mediterranean immigrants, meant that the Catholic Church grew important. Catholics are now the strongest churchgoers, but on paper there are more Anglicans, probably because people of little faith list Anglican on census returns.

Of the other Christian churches, the Uniting Church, joining Methodists and Presbyterians, is one of the strongest. The high proportion of Greeks in Melbourne makes that city a stronghold of the Greek Orthodox Church. The different churches often join together for worship, with large outdoor services on special occasions.

Christians have tried to make their forms of worship relevant to modern Australians. In 1977, an interdenominational Hymn Book modernized the language of many traditional hymns, and removed references that are unrelated to the Southern Hemisphere, like a snowy Christmas.

Other faiths

Successive groups of immigrants have brought other religions with them. The synagogues in Sydney and Melbourne reflect strong Jewish communities. Islam first came to Australia with camel drivers from South Asia and the recent influx of Asians has made Islam relatively strong with mosques in several cities. At lunchtime in the malls of many cities you can often see the Buddhist Hare Krishnas dancing and chanting in their saffron robes.

Aboriginal belief

Long before Europeans arrived in Australia, the Aboriginal people maintained a strong system of beliefs and worship. Indeed, everything traditional Aboriginals do has a religious significance. How to live, they believe, was told to the first people by the Spirit Ancestors, mythical beings with the form of animals or plants or insects, but who behaved like human beings.

According to Aboriginals, the world was created during the Dreamtime, time when things had no form. The Rainbow Snake moved through a desolate landscape. As it twisted and turned, its body created the riverbeds. The earth that it tossed aside became the mountains. The Rainbow Snake gave birth to all the creatures that inhabit the world today.

The Spirit Ancestors moved through this early landscape. Wherever they stopped something happened, they might become a particular hill or rock formation, and Aboriginals speak of these features as being their ancestors. Part of Aboriginal growing up is learning to sing the

AUSTRALIA

These Aboriginals are preparing for a Corroborree. There are different dances for different occasions, such as to celebrate spearing a dangerous crocodile, or as part of a religious ceremony.

song recording what happened to an Ancestor at a particular location.

The paths the Ancestors have taken through the landscape are called the Dreaming Tracks. Today, Aboriginals still follow the Dreaming Tracks, singing the songs appropriate to each landscape feature, each ancestral event. This whole process of walking and singing is called Singing the Dreaming. It embodies a kind of worship, and is used to give meaning to food-gathering and trade with other tribes. The Dreaming Tracks may be 1,000 miles long and will have been walked by many generations of Aboriginals.

To Aboriginals the landscape embodies the Spirit Ancestors of the tribes and they feel a special closeness to it. Aboriginals say, "The earth

THE SKY IS OUR CHURCH

Aboriginal people use the natural surfaces of rock for much of their art. The figures are drawn with charcoal from burnt wood and colored with white chalk and red and yellow ochres. Ochre is clay colored by iron ore. Many of the sites have been used for thousands of years and each generation has a duty to renew the old paintings as well as adding new ones.

is our mother, the sky is our church." When modern developments dig tunnels or mines, Aboriginals feel their mother is being hurt. They may want to stop such activities, particularly if sacred sites are involved. Unfortunately, other Australians sometimes see this religious objection as obstructiveness.

Uluru, or Ayers Rock as it was known to white Australians, is a sacred site of particular importance, with a cave where generations of the *Pitjantjatjara* women have gone to give birth. Parts of Uluru are decorated with Aboriginal rock art, like many other sacred sites. Some of the art consists of beautiful decorative patterns. There are pictures of animals drawn with a careful sense of proportion. Some of these animal pictures are called X-ray art, because the skeleton and the internal organs are shown as well as the external form. Elsewhere, Aboriginal art also records the arrival of European ships and Europeans.

Aboriginal beliefs helped preserve an ecological balance. Each tribe had a totem animal, that it could not kill. For example, members of the emu totem could not kill emus, members of the wallaby totem could not kill wallabies, and so on. Even if animals were not on your totem, you might only kill sufficient for your needs.

The early settlers took little trouble to find out about the Aboriginals' spiritual beliefs; they thought they were savages. Missionaries came to convert the Aboriginals, often dressing them in quite inappropriate European clothes and teaching them to deny the importance of their own culture. The missionaries may have been well-meaning, but the result was to leave Aboriginals with no sense of meaning or purpose.

In contrast, Aboriginals were horrified at the way the Europeans treated each other. In particular, they were amazed at the floggings given to convicts. To Aboriginals, Europeans seemed harsh and unfeeling. It may be that Europeans today can learn from Aboriginal beliefs with their stress on sharing and on the unity between people, animals, environment, and the spiritual aspect of everything.

11 Learning and Caring

By law, all Australian children must go to school between the ages of 6 and 15 (16 in Tasmania). In practice, most children start "kindy" or kindergarten, at four and go to school when they are five. Two-thirds of all children go to state schools where they receive a "free" education. That means that the state pays for their schooling from taxation. One quarter go to Catholic schools, and the remainder to other private schools.

Education then and now

A hundred years ago, school buildings were as primitive as people's homes. Often bush schools had no windows. There were so many cracks

With its clapboard classroom on posts, known as stumps, window awning, and water tank, this is a typical Queensland country school.

between the rough planks that enough light came in to work by. Although the school might be primitive, this did not mean that the children's work was poor. Often it was actually on a very high standard, taught by teachers who had to obey rules every bit as much as children. Teachers had to sign a contract not to smoke or drink, even in their spare time, and they were expected to read the Bible in the evenings. Women teachers were not allowed to marry!

Today a typical school in the outback may only have one or two teachers teaching in a painted wooden building. Sometimes it's raised on stilts, and the space below fitted with seats and drinking fountains to make a cool resting-place. The water comes from a big round tank next to the building. In a primary school there will be swings and slides and, in the dry and sandy outback, maybe even a grasspit — the reverse of a sandbox. Children living in the very distant outback are taught by School of the Air.

Schools in older cities like Sydney can be narrow brick buildings with two or three floors of classrooms. In the modern suburbs schools often spread out over a large area, and classrooms are reached along covered walkways.

State schools are mainly coeducational, with boys and girls taught in the same classrooms. The wide range of countries that immigrants come from means that most city schools are multi-cultural. There can be up to 40 nationalities in one school. Many schools teach children in the language spoken at home, as well as in English.

The growth of an Aboriginal consciousness means that Aboriginal people are now beginning

LEARNING AND CARING

Australian children often enjoy lessons outside. In the country they are often taught about the bush. Here the children are learning where to find honey. In schools near the sea, there are lessons in swimming and life-saving — very important skills in a beach-going nation.

to re-create their own forms of education and caring. There are a few schools that teach aboriginal children about their traditional way of life as well as writing and mathematics.

High School and university

Depending on the state, children start high school at 11 or 12. Italian is often taught in preference to French or German. Increasingly, children learn Asian languages such as Japanese or Indonesian.

When students complete their studies, the school assesses them and the state awards a certificate. Many children stay in school two years more to gain a higher level certificate, usually covering between four and seven main subjects.

Degrees have been available since Sydney

AUSTRALIA

At secondary school, technical studies are an important part of the school day.

University was founded in 1850 and Melbourne University in 1853. Now there are about 20 Australian universities and in addition, a wide range of academic courses are offered in different kinds of colleges.

Health care

Australians are proud of their health care. Hospitals are modern, well-equipped, and well-staffed. As in Britain, people do not have to pay to go into the many public hospitals, but private health care is available for those who wish to pay. Everyone is entitled to have 85 percent of any

LEARNING AND CARING

medical and optician's fees paid for them. This is done through Medicare, a government program.

One hundred years ago, hospitals were little more than places providing a bed to die in. Medical science has improved a great deal and today modern hospitals provide not only cures for many diseases, but preventive care as well. These may involve X-rays to check for early signs of heart diseases or cancers, or blood tests to discover other kinds of disease. More than in many other countries, Australians are aware that prevention is better than cure. The government sponsors health awareness campaigns with slogans like "Life — be in it!"

Welfare
Three-quarters of Australian homes are owned by the people who live in them. (In the United States, it is about 60 percent.) The rest are rented, mainly from private landlords and public housing commissions. This situation means that most Australians go on living in their own home when they retire and get older. Of course, they may sell their homes and move into an apartment rather than a house. The states, churches, and private landlords run housing complexes for the elderly.

Australia was one of the first countries to set up a social security system. From 1910 there have been state retirement pensions, and maternity benefits since 1912. Poor people, and the unemployed, also receive social security payments.

Aboriginal caring
Traditionally, Aboriginal families helped each other out. Food would be shared at any time, and

even distant relatives could expect to be cared for if they were sick or wounded. Old people weren't felt to be a burden, rather they were an important source of wisdom. They might be too old to hunt, but they could pass on their knowledge to the younger members of the tribe.

Many of these patterns have now broken down. Except in the outback, tribal groupings no longer exist to give care, and many Aboriginal people now have to rely on state health and welfare programs. Fortunately, Aboriginals are beginning to band together to get their own clinics and community centers. One example is the Swan Valley settlement outside Perth.

12   Outdoor Lifestyle

The climate, the closeness of Australian cities to the sea, and the large gardens often with swimming pools, all combine to give Australians an outdoor lifestyle.

Barbecues

Eating is often an outside activity, too. Families set up the barbecue next to the pool, and grill delicious steaks, chops, and seafood.

People who live in apartments can take their food to parks where there are public barbecues. A 50-cent piece is put in the slot and the electric hotplate on a brick stand is ready for cooking.

What is hard for the Americans and British to remember is that the main vacation period in Australia is from the end of November to the end of January. This means that Christmas falls in the middle of the summer vacation. Many Australians still eat a traditional English dinner on Christmas Day, except that the turkey is often cold on the beach. Santa Clauses may have a hard time, because they have to dress up when the temperature may be 95°F.

On the beach
Families spend several weeks at one of the many seaside resorts up and down Australia's eastern and southeastern coasts, enjoying the long sandy beaches and the good surf. There are so many miles of beaches, that they are rarely very crowded except close to the cities. More than any other sport, surfing seems to typify Australia. The seas are warm (although not as warm as the Mediterranean) and waves have the whole of the Pacific and Indian Ocean to build up strength before crashing against Australian shores. Rough seas to Australians mean enormous waves 16 — 32 feet high!

As well as enjoying all the fun of the surf, children also learn how to cope with unpleasant experiences like being "barrelled." This is when a treacherous wave suddenly drops you several feet painfully onto the sand.

Surf Carnivals are very Australian. Highly trained volunteer lifesaving teams gather from a number of beaches to hold races and relays. The teams usually have distinctive swimming costumes and special kinds of headgear. These

OUTDOOR LIFESTYLE

Surfing is exciting but it can be dangerous as the seas are often rough. The beaches usually have a team of lifeguards. Sometimes the lifeguards put on a display such as this carnival at Port Noarlunga in South Australia. These carnivals are very popular.

have a practical function in helping the rest of the team to see where a lifesaver has swum with the rope. The teams operate row boats, and learn to become very proficient at all forms of lifesaving. As well as being enjoyable, Surf Carnivals enable the teams to develop their skills to the utmost.

Sharks swim in the seas around Australia. Spotter planes patrol popular coasts and a watch is kept at beaches for the triangular fin. If a shark is sighted, warning bells or sirens sound, and swimmers come tumbling out of the water fast. Bays sometimes have shark nets strung between the headlands, which act as a deterrent. Even so, four or five Australians are attacked every year by sharks.

A common sight on beaches is people with

AUSTRALIA

Australia has the highest skin-cancer rate in the world. To alert people to the danger, there was a big advertising campaign based around the Slip Slop Slap motto: slip on a shirt, slop on some suncream, and slap on a hat. These children protect their faces with pink zinc cream.

colored zinc ointment smeared on their noses and cheeks. Doctors are now sure that too much sunburn increases the likelihood of skin cancers developing as people get older. Fair-skinned people are most at risk.

Into the bush

Besides beach vacations, many families travel in camper vans or go on camping trips into the outback. Few Australians can resist "the lure of

OUTDOOR LIFESTYLE

the bush," and more and more people drive off on long tours of their immense country.

A number of national parks have been created to protect the environment. They have also become tourist attractions, and one of the most famous is Kakadu National Park in the Northern Territory. Covering 5,018 square miles, it varies from crocodile swamps to jungle-like vine-hung cliffs, and is rich in wildlife. Kakadu has a large number of important Aboriginal sites. Its most recent claim to fame is as the site for filming parts of *Crocodile Dundee*.

Kakadu National Park, not far from Darwin, is one of the natural wonders of the world and is home to many tropical species of plants, animals, and birds. This group are out crocodile spotting.

89

The Great Barrier Reef

One of the most outstanding tourist attractions of Australia is the Great Barrier Reef off the coast of Queensland. The Reef is a chain of 500 small islands and coral reefs 2,000 miles long, which makes it the longest coral reef in the world. It is made up of an outer reef that is still growing, and an older inner reef.

The Reef is home to about 400 kinds of coral and 1,500 types of fish. The water is clear and warm. Many tourists enjoy diving and snorkeling to view turtles, stingrays, sea anemones, and starfish. Some of the creatures are dangerous or poisonous such as sharks, coneshells, and jellyfish.

In the 1970s large parts of the Reef were eaten by the crown of thorns starfish, that suddenly increased in numbers. In recent years, however, the starfish population has returned to more normal levels.

Sports

With such an outdoor lifestyle, it is not surprising that Australians are good at sports. In particular Australia produces strong cricket teams and there is a long-standing rivalry with Britain. Additional one-day international matches draw huge crowds.

Soccer and rugby are guaranteed to bring out supporters in droves, flaunting their teams' scarves and colors. In southern Australia, fans go wild over Australian Rules football, played by its own special rules.

In a country where cattle-raising is so important you might expect to find rodeos. Given Australia's climate you might not expect to find skiing. Nevertheless, there is plenty of snow each

OUTDOOR LIFESTYLE

Famous Australian Sportsmen and Sportswomen.

Cricket:	Dennis Lillee, fast bowler
	Greg Chappell, captain
	Sir Donald Bradman
	Richie Benaud
Tennis:	Evonne Cawley (Goolagong) Wimbledon champion 1980
	Pat Cash, Rod Laver, John Newcombe, Margaret Court
Swimming:	Dawn Fraser, 4 Olympic Gold Medals 1956–64
Golf:	Greg Norman
	Bruce Devlin
Squash:	Geoffrey Hunt, Men's world champion 1976–77, 1979–80
	Heather Mckay (Blundell) women's world champion 1976 and 1979
Auto Racing:	Jack Brabham, world champion 1959, 1960, and 1966

winter on the Australian Alps between Melbourne and Sydney and skiiers become proficient at down hill and cross-country.

The outdoor lifestyle from days in the surf to evenings on the veranda is the essence of being Australian. However, there is much more to Australia. This book should help get rid of myths such as "all Australians live on sheep stations in the outback," or "Australia was uninhabited until the First Fleet arrived." Australia today is a prosperous, mainly urban society, democratic, and with a rich mix of cultures. It is beginning to

AUSTRALIA

Most forms of outside sport are popular in Australia as the weather is ideal for it. Both cricket and Australian Rules football attract large crowds.

OUTDOOR LIFESTYLE

realize the importance of the Aboriginal people's culture and the lessons to be learned from their harmony with the environment. It is a country full of promise for the people who live there.

> **Australian Rules football** is a game that began in the Australian goldfields in the 1880s. It is widely played in Australia, but is particularly popular in the state of Victoria. There are 18 players on each team who play with an oval ball, punching it instead of throwing it. In this fast open game the players may run with the ball as long as they bounce it every 10 yards. There are four goalposts without crossbars at each end. If a goal is kicked between the two inner posts six points are scored. If the ball goes between an inner and outer post only one point is scored.

Index

Aboriginal people 19, 20, 24, 25, 26, 27, 30, 37, 53
   arts 36
   education 80, 81
   housing 48
   land rights 55, 72, 73
   lifestyle 47, 48, 92
   religion 75, 76, 77, 78
   welfare, 83, 84
Adelaide 31, 39, 41, 42, 49, 63, 64, 70
air travel 34, 41, 42, 43
animals 10, 14, 16, 18, 19, 20, 26, 41, 51
Anzacs (Australian and New Zealand Army Corps) 32
Ayers Rock (Uluru) 8, 73, 77

Ballarat 28, 52
Banks, Sir Joseph 22
Bass Strait 57
Bathurst 28, 52
Bendigo 28
Blue Mountains 9, 24
Botany Bay 22, 60, 61
Brisbane 12, 31, 49, 63
Brisbane River 63
Britain 33, 34, 38, 57
Broken Hill 53
Burke, Robert 41, 42
bush 9, 14, 24
   fires 12
bushrangers 30

Canberra 32, 36, 62, 63
   climate 6, 9, 10, 11, 13, 49, 62, 63, 66
   rainfall 9, 10, 11, 12, 13
convicts 22, 23, 24, 25, 27, 30, 63, 78
Cook, Captain James 21, 22
currency 4, 24
cyclones 11
   Cyclone Tracy 12, 65

Darling River 7, 10, 38, 48
Darwin 12, 42, 65
desert 9, 10, 13, 20, 41, 42
dust storms 12

Echuca 39
ecology 48, 49, 78
education 45, 46, 79, 80, 81, 82
   distance learning 45, 46, 80
   higher 81, 82
   kindergarten 79
   primary 79, 80
   secondary 81
energy 54
   coal 57
   gas 57
   hydroelectricity 58
   oil 57
equator 6, 9
Eyre, Edward 41

farming 23, 24, 44, 50, 51
   crops 50, 51
   sheep 25, 26, 27, 39, 44, 45, 51

films 18, 89, 34, 35, 36, 89
First Fleet 23
floods 12
Flying Doctor Service 46
Fremantle 65

government 31, 32, 71, 72
   Federation 32, 71
Great Barrier Reef 19, 90
Great Dividing Range 7, 8
Great Victoria Desert 13
Gulf of Carpentaria 42
gum trees 12, 14

health and welfare 46, 47, 82, 83
Hobart 6, 65
housing 48, 52, 66, 67, 68

immigrants 19, 24, 50, 68, 70, 80

Japan 6, 34, 35, 43, 57, 58

Kalgoorlie 41
Kelly, Ned 30

Labor and Trade Union
   Movement 28, 29
Lake Eyre 7, 11
language 68, 69, 80, 81
lifestyle 12, 66, 85, 86, 92
literature 35, 36

marsupials 14, 16, 17, 18, 20, 26
Melbourne 12, 30, 31, 32, 39, 40, 61, 62

Melbourne University 82
minerals and mining 8, 27, 28, 29, 43, 52, 53, 54, 55, 57
motor transportation 38
   cars 33
mountains 6, 7, 8, 9, 24
Murray River 10, 38, 39, 49, 58
Murrumbidgee River 10, 58
music 36

national parks 89
   Kakadu National Park 89
New Guinea 6, 19, 35
New South Wales 28, 31, 49, 53, 57
New Zealand 6, 32
Newman 55, 56
Northern Territory 8, 31, 54, 65
North West Shelf 57
nuclear weapons 73
Nullarbor Plain 41

Olgas 8
outback 9, 47, 48

Pacific Ocean 5, 35, 86
Perth 32, 41, 49, 64, 73
Phillip, Captain Arthur 23, 60
population 9, 61
Port Augusta 41
Port Elliot 39
Port Hedland 55, 57
Port Jackson 23
possum 16, 17

Queensland 6, 18, 19, 31, 39, 49, 50, 53, 57, 63

radio 34, 42
railroads 32, 39, 40, 41
　trans-Australia 41
religion 74, 75, 76, 77, 78
　Aboriginal 75, 76, 77, 78
　Christianity 74
　other faiths 75
Riverina 51
rivers 7, 10, 11, 41, 58, 62, 63
road travel 37, 38, 41

Sandridge 39
savannah 9, 13, 25
School of the Air 45, 46, 80
Snowy Mountains Project 57, 58
South Australia 12, 31, 54, 63
sports 62, 91, 93
　car racing 64, 91
　cricket 91
　skiing 92
　soccer and rugby 91, 93
　surfing 86, 87, 93
　yachting 65
Strangeray Springs 44
Sturts Desert 13
Swan River 64, 65
Sydney 5, 23, 39, 40, 42, 57, 59, 60, 61
Sydney Opera House 36

Tasmania (Van Diemen's Land) 6, 13, 18, 19, 27, 51, 53, 65

telegraph 42
television 36
time 5
　Australian daylight savings 5
　U.S. daylight savings 5
Torres Strait 49
trade 19, 34, 37, 39, 43, 44
　exports 44, 48, 49, 57
tropics 42

Uluru (Ayers Rock) 8, 73, 77
United States 5, 33, 35, 48, 57, 58

vacations 86, 88, 89
Van Diemen's Land 31
Victoria 12, 14, 28, 31, 50, 57

war 32, 33
　Vietnam 35
　World War I 32, 33
　World War II 43, 70
Wentworth, William 25
Western Australia 31, 41, 53, 64, 65
wildlife 10, 13, 16, 17, 18, 19, 20, 26, 41, 51
　birds 14, 15, 18
　fish 19
　plants 10, 12, 13, 14, 25
　reptiles 18
　sharks 87
Wills, William 41, 42
writers 35

Yarra River 62